STARS AND PLANETS

Text/Consultant: Dr. John O'Byrne
Illustrator: Robert Mancini

Published by
The National Geographic Society
Reg Murphy, President and Chief Executive Officer
Gilbert M. Grosvenor, Chairman of the Board
Nina D. Hoffman, Senior Vice President
William R. Gray, Vice President and Director, Book Division
Barbara Lalicki, Director of Children's Publishing
Barbara Brownell, Senior Editor
Mark A. Caraluzzi, Marketing Manager
Vincent P. Ryan, Manufacturing Manager

Library of Congress Catalog Number: 96-06849
ISBN: 0-7922-3450-2

Produced for the National Geographic Society by Weldon Owen Pty Ltd
43 Victoria Street, McMahons Point, NSW 2060, Australia
A member of the Weldon Owen Group of Companies
Sydney • San Francisco

President: John Owen
Publisher: Sheena Coupe
Project Editor: Jenni Bruce
Text Editor: Robert Coupe
Assistant Editor: Elizabeth Connolly
Art Director: Sue Burk
Designer: Mark Thacker
Photo Researcher: Amanda Weir
Production Manager: Caroline Webber

Film production by Mandarin Offset
Printed in Mexico

MY FIRST
POCKET
GUIDE

STARS AND
PLANETS

DR. JOHN O'BYRNE

NATIONAL
GEOGRAPHIC
SOCIETY

INTRODUCTION

After the Sun slips below the horizon at night, the sky slowly darkens to reveal twinkling stars and glowing planets. Can you spot the planet Venus as it rises? Do you know where to find the stars that make up the pattern of Orion, the Hunter? Become a skywatcher and show these sights to your family and friends!

City lights can make faint stars hard to find, but even in the city there is plenty to see in the night sky. Wherever you are, you can watch the parade of stars changing as the hours pass. The brighter planets—our nearby neighbors—stand out in the sky. They seem to move slowly among the stars.

With binoculars or a telescope, you can really begin to explore the wonders of the Universe. Faint planets and their moons become clearer. Clusters of colored stars sparkle like jewels. Vast galaxies look like delicate clouds among the stars.

HOW TO USE THIS BOOK

Most spreads in this book help you to identify something you might see in the night sky. A picture at the start of each spread shows what you can expect to see. The text explains what features to look for and tells how big and how far away the object is. The "Field Notes" give an unusual fact. The book has three parts: **Our Solar System,** with objects such as planets and meteors; **The Universe,** with more distant objects such as stars and galaxies; and **Constellations,** which are patterns of stars in our sky. At the end of the book, there are star charts to help you find your way around the night sky. If you spot a word you don't know, look it up in the Glossary on page 76.

EXPLORING SPACE

We live on a planet called Earth. It may seem enormous to us, but compared to the rest of the Universe, it is tiny. Earth is just one of nine planets in our Solar System, which is a small part of the Milky Way Galaxy. The Milky Way is just one of the billions of galaxies that are scattered throughout the Universe!

Telescopes can help you see the light that comes from stars and planets. Because the stars are so far away, you will see only a tiny point of light when you look at a star through a telescope. The planets are much closer. A telescope will show you a small disk, which is one side of the planet.

Astronomers are people who study the Universe. They use huge telescopes to see distant stars and galaxies. They even

These radio telescopes are shaped like dishes to help them pick up radio waves from stars and galaxies.

have satellite telescopes, which travel through space. Stars give off many different kinds of light, including light that people usually can't see. Special telescopes sense infrared light, which is just heat. Others detect ultraviolet light—the sort that can give you sunburn when it comes from the Sun. Astronomers also use radio telescopes to investigate invisible radio waves that come from stars and galaxies.

There is no oxygen in space. Astronauts must wear special suits so they can breathe.

Astronauts are people who travel into space. Some have walked on the Moon and brought back rocks from its surface. Scientists also use robot spacecraft—ones without astronauts aboard—that send back pictures of the planets. In the future, people may be able to live on special bases on some planets or moons, or in a space station in space. Travel to the stars seems beyond our reach, but we can still learn a lot about the Universe by viewing it from Earth.

The biggest planets in our Solar System are Saturn (front left) and Jupiter (middle).

OUR SOLAR SYSTEM

A solar system is a group of planets, asteroids, comets, and dust, all moving around a central star and following paths called orbits. Gravity from the star holds them on these orbits.

Almost five billion years ago, our Solar System formed out of a swirling cloud of gas and dust. It has nine planets orbiting the Sun—its only star.

From nearest to farthest from the Sun, the nine planets are: Mercury, Venus, Earth, Mars, Jupiter, Saturn, Uranus, Neptune, and Pluto. Planets don't shine like the Sun, but you can see them because they reflect the Sun's light. They are constantly moving, so it is hard to say where they will be from night to night, but if you see a bright "star" that is not on the star charts at the end of this book, it is probably a nearby planet.

Just as the Sun is orbited by planets, some of the planets are orbited by small moons. Earth's own Moon is easy to see in the sky at night. Many planets and moons have craters—scars left by asteroids, comets, and meteorites that have crashed into them.

Distances between the planets are vast. If a jet aircraft could fly through space, it would take two weeks to reach the Moon. If the space shuttle could fly to the Moon at its fastest speed, it would arrive in less than a day. But even the shuttle would take almost 30 years to reach Pluto.

The space shuttle would take at least 100,000 years to reach any star beyond our Solar System.

THE SUN

Like all stars, the Sun is a giant ball of gas. At its center, the temperature is millions of degrees. Even the surface is 10,000°F—so hot that only gas can exist there.

HOW BIG AND HOW FAR?

EARTH

SUN

The Sun is more than 100 times bigger than Earth, but looks only about as big as the Moon in our sky. This is because it is so far away—about 93 million miles.

WHAT YOU WILL SEE:

WARNING Never look directly at the Sun, especially through a telescope or binoculars. You could go blind!

✳ **WITH YOUR EYES**
The Sun is too bright to look at.
✳ **THROUGH A TELESCOPE**
Never look at it through a telescope. Use only the method in the "Field Notes."
✳ **IF YOU COULD GET CLOSER**
You would see the boiling surface gases.

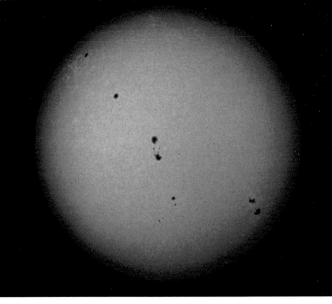

Cooler, darker patches sometimes appear on the surface of the Sun. They are called sunspots.

FIELD NOTES

The only safe way to look at the Sun is to let it shine through a telescope onto a white card.

MERCURY

The planet closest to the Sun, Mercury, has no air to protect it from the Sun's heat. The sunny side can get as hot as 750°F, but the dark side can be as cold as 360°F below freezing.

This picture shows Mercury's craters. It was taken from the Mariner 10 spacecraft.

HOW BIG AND HOW FAR?

MERCURY

EARTH

Mercury is less than half the size of Earth and is 36 million miles from the Sun. A space shuttle would take almost three months to fly from the Sun to Mercury.

WHAT YOU WILL SEE:

✳ WITH YOUR EYES
To find Mercury, look for a "star" near the horizon just after sunset or before sunrise. It can be hard to see because it stays close to the Sun in the sky.

✳ THROUGH A TELESCOPE
Sometimes Mercury can look like a tiny crescent shape.

✳ IF YOU COULD GET CLOSER
Craters cover Mercury's surface.

FIELD NOTES

From Mercury, the Sun would look three times bigger than it looks from Earth—and much brighter.

VENUS

The superhot, rocky surface of Venus is always covered by a mass of clouds. These clouds reflect the light of the Sun, which is why Venus looks like the brightest "star" in our sky.

HOW BIG AND HOW FAR?

VENUS

EARTH

Venus is almost the same size as Earth. It is 70 million miles from the Sun. As it orbits the Sun, it comes closer to Earth than any other planet.

WHAT YOU WILL SEE:

✳ WITH YOUR EYES
At different times of year, you can see Venus as the "morning star" at sunrise or the "evening star" at sunset.

✳ THROUGH A TELESCOPE
It often looks like a small white crescent.

✳ IF YOU COULD GET CLOSER
You would be very hot! The thick air and clouds trap heat, giving Venus the hottest surface in our Solar System.

Venus's clouds are made of acid. The clouds above Earth are made of water.

FIELD NOTES

Pictures of Venus show rocky ground dimly lit by the orange glow of the Sun shining through clouds.

EARTH

Because of its distance from the Sun, Earth is just the right temperature for water to exist as a liquid—making it the only planet with oceans, lakes, and rivers on the surface. Earth is also the only planet with oxygen in its air.

Astronauts see Earth as a delicate, colorful ball floating in space.

HOW BIG AND HOW FAR?

EARTH
SUN

Our planet is nearly 8,000 miles wide. Light from the Sun takes about 8 minutes to travel the 93 million miles to Earth. Earth takes one year to orbit the Sun.

WHAT YOU WILL SEE:

✳ WITH YOUR EYES
The plants, animals, and people that you see on Earth are special things you would not see on other planets.

✳ THROUGH A TELESCOPE
At night, you can study all the stars and planets in the sky.

✳ IF YOU COULD GET FAR AWAY
From space, you would see Earth's vast oceans, swirling clouds, and landmasses.

FIELD NOTES

The plants and animals that live on Earth need oxygen and water to survive.

THE MOON

Like other moons, Earth's Moon is covered with craters made by meteorites that crashed into its surface. The craters range from a few feet across to hundreds of miles across.

Astronauts landed on the Moon in a small spacecraft called a lunar module.

Moon

Sun

TOTAL ECLIPSE

HOW BIG AND HOW FAR?

MOON

EARTH

Earth is almost four times bigger than the Moon. But the Moon looks big to us because it is only 240,000 miles away—closer than most other objects in space.

WHAT YOU WILL SEE:

✳ WITH YOUR EYES
Depending on where the Moon is in its orbit around Earth, you will see a crescent, a half disk, or a "full" Moon.

✳ THROUGH A TELESCOPE
You can see craters, mountains, and valleys. Learn some of their names by looking at the maps on pages 20 and 21.

✳ IF YOU COULD GET CLOSER
You would walk on a powdery surface.

FIELD NOTES

A solar eclipse is when the Moon moves in front of the Sun, casting a shadow on part of Earth.

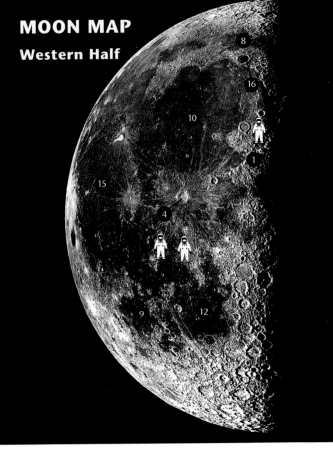

MOON MAP

Western Half

These two half-disk photographs of the Moon show its rough craters and mountains and its smooth seas. A sea on the Moon does not contain any water. It is called a "mare," which means "sea" in Latin. The shadows you see when the Moon is a half disk or a crescent make its features more obvious.

The Voyager I spacecraft took this photograph of Jupiter from 22 million miles away.

FIELD NOTES

Jupiter's closest moon, Io (EYE-oh), is scattered with volcanoes that shoot out plumes of gas and dust.

25

SATURN

Through a telescope, the splendid rings of Saturn look like three separate rings. Close-up photographs show that there are actually hundreds of narrow "ringlets." Saturn is made mostly of gas and covered by clouds.

FIELD NOTES

The rings are made of millions of icy rocks circling Saturn. Some of the rocks are as big as houses.

As Saturn
orbits the Sun,
its rings can be seen
from changing angles.

HOW BIG AND HOW FAR?

SATURN

EARTH

Saturn is 900 million miles from the Sun. That makes it 10 times farther away from the Sun than Earth is. It is almost 10 times bigger than Earth.

WHAT YOU WILL SEE:

✳ WITH YOUR EYES
Saturn looks like a yellowish star that moves even more slowly than Jupiter.

✳ THROUGH A TELESCOPE
The rings are easy to see, except every 13 years, when their angle to Earth makes them seem to disappear.

✳ IF YOU COULD GET CLOSER
You would see that "ringlets" fill what usually looks like a dark gap in the rings.

URANUS

Uranus, far out in our Solar System, was discovered by an English astronomer only 200 years ago. It is smaller and colder than Jupiter and Saturn, but with the same thick atmosphere.

HOW BIG AND HOW FAR?

URANUS
EARTH

Uranus is 4 times bigger than Earth. The Sun's light takes almost 3 hours to travel the 1,700 million miles to the planet, in the cold, outer parts of our Solar System.

WHAT YOU WILL SEE:

＊WITH YOUR EYES
You may just see Uranus in a very dark sky. It is a faint point of light.

＊THROUGH A TELESCOPE
Even through a telescope, Uranus looks like a tiny, blue-green disk without any obvious markings.

＊IF YOU COULD GET CLOSER
You would see how Uranus's thin rings are made up of thousands of icy rocks.

Uranus is circled by 15 icy moons.
Here you see the largest of them.

NEPTUNE

The most distant planet that any spacecraft has visited is Neptune. Like the other giant planets, it is circled by moons with ancient craters all over their icy surfaces.

The Voyager 2 spacecraft took this photograph. It shows white clouds around a giant storm that looks like a dark spot.

HOW BIG AND HOW FAR?

NEPTUNE

EARTH

Neptune is more than 30,000 miles across, which is almost as big as Uranus. It is 2,800 million miles from the Sun—30 times farther away than Earth is.

WHAT YOU WILL SEE:

✳ WITH YOUR EYES
Neptune is too faint to see.
✳ THROUGH A TELESCOPE
It is very hard to find, but if you do, you'll see just a tiny disk, even smaller than Uranus, but with a bluish tinge.
✳ IF YOU COULD GET CLOSER
You would see dark, stormy spots and bright, icy clouds floating in Neptune's blue atmosphere.

FIELD NOTES

The planets are named after ancient Roman gods. Neptune was god of the sea.

PLUTO

No spacecraft has yet reached Pluto, the smallest and most distant planet in our Solar System. Pluto has only one moon. It is called Charon (KAIR-on) and takes about six days to circle the planet.

FIELD NOTES
Walt Disney's cartoon dog Pluto first appeared soon after the planet Pluto was sighted in 1930.

HOW BIG AND HOW FAR?

Pluto is 5 times smaller than Earth—even smaller than Earth's Moon. It moves around the Sun in a football-shaped orbit. Other planets have almost circular orbits.

WHAT YOU WILL SEE:

✳ WITH YOUR EYES
Pluto is much too faint to see.

✳ THROUGH A TELESCOPE
The only way to find Pluto is to watch its very slow movement across the starry sky. It will look like a very faint star.

✳ IF YOU COULD GET CLOSER
Pluto and Charon would probably be cold and icy and covered with craters, like some of Neptune's moons.

Charon is half the size of Pluto and is very close to the planet.

33

METEOR AND METEORITE

People often call meteors (MEET-ee-uhrs) shooting stars, but they are really tiny rocks from space that burn up in a flash when they enter Earth's atmosphere. Meteorites are bigger rocks that reach the ground.

A meteor flashes across the sky against the glow of a distant aurora.

HOW BIG AND HOW FAR?

Most meteors are like tiny grains or pebbles, but meteorites can be bigger than a football. Meteors usually burn up and disappear about 50 miles above the ground.

WHAT YOU WILL SEE:

✴ WITH YOUR EYES
In dark places, you can see a meteor flash every few minutes. When many meteors come from one patch of sky, it is called a meteor shower.

✴ THROUGH A TELESCOPE
Meteors travel too fast for you to see them through a telescope or binoculars.

✴ IF YOU COULD GET CLOSER
A meteor might hit your spacecraft!

FIELD NOTES

Some meteorites make craters in the ground when they land. A few have even crashed into cars!

ASTEROID

Asteroids are pieces of rock that circle the Sun like tiny planets. Some have orbits that occasionally bring them close to Earth. If an asteroid ever hits Earth, it will make a huge crater.

HOW BIG AND HOW FAR?

CERES

EARTH

The biggest asteroid, Ceres (SEER-eez), is 600 miles across, but most are just a few miles across. The asteroid belt is 260 million miles from the Sun.

WHAT YOU WILL SEE:

✴ WITH YOUR EYES
Even bright ones are too faint to see.

✴ THROUGH A TELESCOPE
Because they are so small, asteroids look like stars. You can pick them out as they move in the sky from one night to the next.

✴ IF YOU COULD GET CLOSER
You would see asteroids of various shapes, all with cratered surfaces.

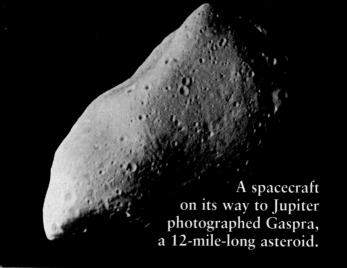

A spacecraft on its way to Jupiter photographed Gaspra, a 12-mile-long asteroid.

FIELD NOTES

Most asteroids move around the Sun between Mars and Jupiter. People call this area the asteroid belt.

COMET

Comets are chunks of rock and ice that orbit the Sun. A comet can be seen only if it goes near the Sun. The heat melts the ice, making a cloudy head and a tail of gas and dust.

HOW BIG AND HOW FAR?

A comet's icy center is only a few miles across, but it produces a huge head and a tail millions of miles long. For most comets, this tail lasts only a few months.

WHAT YOU WILL SEE:

✳ WITH YOUR EYES
To see a comet, find a dark place, well away from city lights.

✳ THROUGH A TELESCOPE
It is easier to see a comet through a pair of binoculars than through a telescope. Watch each night for changes in the tail as the comet's center slowly boils away.

✳ IF YOU COULD GET CLOSER
It would look like a big, dirty snowball.

Comet West's tail split into two, forming a blue gas tail and a whitish dust tail.

FIELD NOTES
In 1994, Comet Shoemaker-Levy 9 hit Jupiter. About every 1,000 years, a comet hits a large planet.

AURORA

Fiery eruptions on the Sun sometimes send particles of gas hurtling out into space toward Earth. When they enter Earth's atmosphere, they create glowing curtains of light, called auroras (uh-ROAR-uhs), in our sky.

Auroras are most often green, but can sometimes have blue and red mixed in.

HOW BIG AND HOW FAR?

Auroras occur 60 miles or more above the ground, usually in a circle around the North and South Poles. They are often seen in Alaska and other northern places.

WHAT YOU WILL SEE:

✴ WITH YOUR EYES
Some auroras are just faint glows, but others form beautiful, sweeping shapes that quiver across the sky.

✴ THROUGH A TELESCOPE
An aurora spreads too far across the sky to be seen well through a telescope.

✴ IF YOU COULD GET CLOSER
You would find that an aurora is a very faint glow spread out through the air.

FIELD NOTES
From space, you could see how an aurora stretches into the highest parts of Earth's atmosphere.

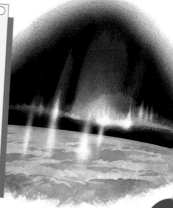

THE UNIVERSE

Beyond our Solar System is the rest of the Milky Way Galaxy, which contains at least a hundred billion stars like our Sun. Many of these stars may have planets that make up their own solar systems. Some stars are buried in clouds of gas. Others are members of groups called star clusters.

Beyond the Milky Way are billions of other galaxies, which are grouped into clusters of galaxies, and even clusters of clusters. They are impossible to count—like grains of sand scattered through space.

Where did these galaxies come from? Most astronomers think that the Universe began in the Big Bang— a gigantic explosion about 15 billion years ago. Since then, the Universe has been expanding, carrying the clusters of galaxies away from each other.

Astronomers often measure the vast

The Hubble Space Telescope is finding many more galaxies.

This photograph was taken by the Hubble Space Telescope. Each speck of light in it is a galaxy.

distances in the Universe in light years. One light year is the distance light travels in a year—about 6,000 billion miles. It is easier to say that Alpha Centauri, the nearest star to our Solar System, is 4.3 light years away, than to say it is 26,000 billion miles away.

Many interesting objects in the sky were listed 200 years ago by an astronomer, Charles Messier. He numbered some 100 galaxies, nebulas, and star clusters in the order in which he saw them. The Pleiades (PLEE-uh-deez) star cluster, for example, is also known as M45. The "M" stands for "Messier." The cluster was the 45th object he saw. Some of these numbers are on the star charts at the end of this book.

STAR CLUSTER

Unlike the Sun, most stars have other stars nearby. When two stars are close together, the pair is called a double star. Hundreds or thousands of stars near each other form a group called a star cluster.

FIELD NOTES

Double stars that are very close together may pull each other out of shape and even share their gas.

HOW BIG AND HOW FAR?

GLOBULAR

OPEN

The biggest clusters are globular clusters. They can be 100 light years across and contain millions of stars. Some of them are more than 100,000 light years away.

WHAT YOU WILL SEE:

✳ WITH YOUR EYES
A star cluster can be hard to see, but will usually look like a fuzzy star.

✳ THROUGH A TELESCOPE
You will see that an open cluster is a loose grouping of stars. A globular cluster is a tight ball of stars.

✳ IF YOU COULD GET CLOSER
In a globular cluster, you would be surrounded by millions of blazing stars.

The Pleiades (M45) is an open cluster. It is seen in the constellation of Taurus, the Bull

NEBULA

Nebulas (NEB-yuh-luhs) are big clouds of gas and dust among the stars. Many nebulas are places where new stars are being born. Others are places where old stars have exploded.

HOW BIG AND HOW FAR?

In many nebulas, the bright part is where new stars are born. It can be several light years across. The rest of the nebula is a much larger cloud of dark gas and dust.

WHAT YOU WILL SEE:

✳ **WITH YOUR EYES**
You can just see a few of the brightest nebulas. The easiest one to see is the Great Nebula (M42) in the constellation of Orion, the Hunter.

✳ **THROUGH A TELESCOPE**
Bright nebulas look like fuzzy clouds.

✳ **IF YOU COULD GET CLOSER**
You may not know you were in a nebula because up close the gas is too thin to see.

M16 is a stunning combination of a nebula, called the Eagle Nebula, and a star cluster.

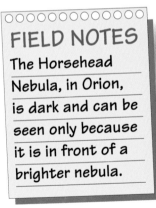

FIELD NOTES

The Horsehead Nebula, in Orion, is dark and can be seen only because it is in front of a brighter nebula.

SUPERNOVA

When a star gets old, its temperature drops and it becomes a red giant star. If it is very big, the star will eventually explode. This explosion is called a supernova. Part of the star might be left behind as a black hole.

Disk of gas

Black hole

A supernova produces an enormous burst of light that lasts for many days.

HOW BIG AND HOW FAR?

BEFORE

AFTER

Before becoming a supernova, a star is much bigger than the Sun. A black hole is only a few miles wide, but it contains more matter than the Sun.

WHAT YOU WILL SEE:

✳ WITH YOUR EYES
Supernovas that you can see without a telescope are very rare. There was one in 1987, the first in almost 400 years.

✳ THROUGH A TELESCOPE
You couldn't see a black hole, but you might see a supernova.

✳ IF YOU COULD GET CLOSER
In a supernova, you would see most of the star's gas blast off into space.

MILKY WAY

Almost all the stars, star clusters, and nebulas that you can see with your eyes or through a small telescope belong to the Milky Way Galaxy, the family of stars that includes the Sun.

FIELD NOTES
By studying where stars are in the sky, scientists know the Milky Way has a central bulge and spiral arms.

Dark dust clouds block our view of the central bulge of the Milky Way.

HOW BIG AND HOW FAR?

OUR SOLAR SYSTEM

The Milky Way contains at least a hundred billion stars. Even if you could travel at the speed of light, you would need more than 30,000 years to reach its center.

WHAT YOU WILL SEE:

✳ WITH YOUR EYES
In a dark sky, the Milky Way appears as a faint, broad band of stars.

✳ THROUGH A TELESCOPE
You can see masses of stars, as well as some nearby star clusters and nebulas.

✳ IF YOU COULD GET CLOSER
If you traveled to the center of the Milky Way, you might find an enormous black hole, a million times bigger than the Sun.

GALAXY

A galaxy is a family of billions of stars. Many galaxies are grouped into galaxy clusters. The Milky Way Galaxy belongs to a cluster known as the Local Group.

HOW BIG AND HOW FAR?

ANDROMEDA

MILKY WAY

More than 2 million light years from Earth is the Andromeda (an-DROM-uh-duh) Galaxy (M31). It contains about 200 billion stars, twice as many as the Milky Way.

WHAT YOU WILL SEE:

✳ WITH YOUR EYES
In a dark sky, you can see a few galaxies, including the Andromeda Galaxy.

✳ THROUGH A TELESCOPE
Most galaxies are hard to see and look small and faint.

✳ IF YOU COULD GET CLOSER
You could explore the Local Group, where astronomers have found nearly 30 galaxies, mostly small elliptical ones.

The Andromeda Galaxy is the nearest big galaxy to the Milky Way.

Spiral

Elliptical

Irregular

CONSTELLATIONS

Since ancient times, people have looked up at the sky and seen patterns in the stars. Some of the patterns are named after people or animals in myths—such as Orion, the Hunter, and Cygnus, the Swan. You must use your imagination to see how the patterns resemble their names, as the artist did below. Today, astronomers divide the sky that we see into 88 areas called constellations. These areas include not only the old patterns of stars, but also distant star clusters, nebulas, and galaxies.

As you watch the night sky, the stars may seem to move in circles. In fact, it is Earth that is moving, slowly spinning around. When your part of the world is facing away from the Sun, at night, you can see stars in the sky.

Three bright stars form the belt of Orion, the Hunter.

The stars in a constellation pattern aren't in a tight group like the stars in a cluster. They are so far apart that you couldn't find the constellation if you were traveling through space.

Five easily seen constellations are described in the next five spreads. Look inside the

This special photograph was taken over many hours to show circular "star trails."

back cover to find out how to judge the size of the constellations with your hands. Each spread has hand symbols to guide you.

To find fainter constellations, you can use the star charts at the end of this book and have fun "star-hopping." There are four charts because the stars that we see change during the year as Earth orbits the Sun. When using a star chart, it helps to find the brightest stars first. Depending on the time of night, the stars may not be exactly where the chart shows, but they will be close by.

URSA MAJOR

The constellation of Ursa (ER-suh) Major, the Great Bear, includes the famous group of stars called the Big Dipper. It also contains M81, one of the closest spiral galaxies to Earth.

HOW BIG AND HOW FAR?

M81

Ursa Major is one of the largest constellations—even with two hands spread, you can't cover it all. The M81 Galaxy is 7 million light years away.

WHAT YOU WILL SEE:

✴ WITH YOUR EYES
The Big Dipper stars—Ursa Major's brightest—are easy to see at most times.

✴ THROUGH A TELESCOPE
The Owl Nebula (M97) is near the Big Dipper. It looks like a faint owl's face.

✴ IF YOU COULD GET CLOSER
The stars Mizar and Alcor would be very far apart, even though they look close together in the Big Dipper's handle.

The stars of Ursa Major have been made brighter in this picture. You can see the Big Dipper on the left side of the pattern.

○○○○○○○○○○○○○○○

FIELD NOTES

Two stars in the Big Dipper point to Polaris, or Pole Star, also called North Star. This marks the way north.

CASSIOPEIA

Polaris

LITTLE DIPPER

N

BIG DIPPER

NORTH

ORION

In winter, look south to see Orion (uh-RYE-uhn), the Hunter. This constellation includes two supergiants—the blue star Rigel (RI-juhl) and the red star Betelgeuse (BEET-uhl-joose).

FIELD NOTES

Looking at Orion, you can find the stunning Great Nebula (M42)—one of the easiest nebulas to see.

Can you see
the three stars
that make up
Orion's belt?

HOW BIG AND HOW FAR?

Most of Orion's bright stars are about 1,500 light years away from Earth. Only Betelgeuse is much closer. It is just 300 light years away from Earth.

WHAT YOU WILL SEE:

✳ WITH YOUR EYES
Between Rigel and Betelgeuse are the three bright stars of Orion's belt, with the sword hanging below.

✳ THROUGH A TELESCOPE
A fuzzy reddish star beneath Orion's belt is revealed to be the Great Nebula.

✳ IF YOU COULD GET CLOSER
You would discover that the Horsehead Nebula is a cold, dusty gas cloud.

LEO

Look south in spring to see Leo, the Lion. It will be high in the sky, standing out against the fainter stars. This constellation is especially clear in cities, where dim stars are hard to see.

HOW BIG AND HOW FAR?

Regulus

You can almost cover Leo with one hand. Leo contains the bluish white star Regulus (REG-you-lus), one of the brightest stars in the sky. It is only 75 light years away.

WHAT YOU WILL SEE:

✳ **WITH YOUR EYES**
The "backward question mark" in Leo also looks like a lion's head and mane.

✳ **THROUGH A TELESCOPE**
Look for spiral galaxies such as M65 and M66.

✳ **IF YOU COULD GET CLOSER**
You could see that when R Leonis, a star near Regulus, changes in brightness, it is also getting larger or smaller.

Can you see the backward question mark with Regulus at the end?

FIELD NOTES
Every November, meteors "rain" out of the sky around Leo's stars. This is called the Leonid meteor shower.

CYGNUS

The constellation of Cygnus (SIG-nus), the Swan, is shaped like a cross. You will find it in one of the brightest parts of the Milky Way, which is nearly overhead in summer.

Cygnus is also called the Northern Cross.

HOW BIG AND HOW FAR?

Cygnus's brightest star is Deneb. Although it is 1,500 light years away, it is very bright in our sky because it is 60,000 times brighter than the Sun.

WHAT YOU WILL SEE:

✷ WITH YOUR EYES
Find Deneb and two other bright stars outside Cygnus—Vega and Altair. The three are called the Summer Triangle.

✷ THROUGH A TELESCOPE
Near Deneb is the open star cluster M39, best seen through binoculars.

✷ IF YOU COULD GET CLOSER
If you went to the Milky Way in Cygnus, you'd be in a spiral arm of the galaxy.

FIELD NOTES

Near Deneb is the North America Nebula, so named because it looks a bit like a map of North America.

PEGASUS

You can recognize Pegasus (PEG-uh-sus), the Winged Horse, because some of its stars form a large square—the Great Square of Pegasus. This constellation passes overhead in fall.

The bright stars of Pegasus stand out clearly in a fairly dim patch of sky.

HOW BIG AND HOW FAR?

You can cover the stars of Pegasus with two spread hands. At one end of the constellation lies the globular star cluster M15, which is 34,000 light years away.

WHAT YOU WILL SEE:

✳ WITH YOUR EYES
Just off one corner of the Great Square, you might see the faint patch of the Andromeda Galaxy (M31).
✳ THROUGH A TELESCOPE
Look for the spectacular globular cluster M15.
✳ IF YOU COULD GET CLOSER
You'd see how the galaxies in Stephan's Quintet pull each other out of shape.

STAR CHARTS

charts for February 15, 9 p.m.

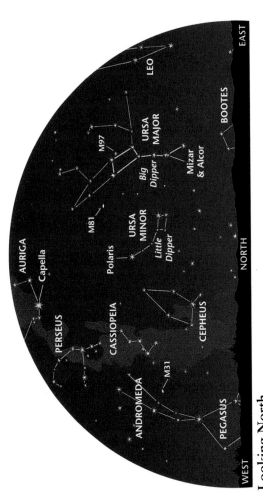

Looking North

The Big Dipper is rising in the northeast. The fainter Little Dipper seems to hang from Polaris. In the west, Perseus, the Hero, is above Cassiopeia, the Queen. Overhead, Capella marks Auriga, the Charioteer.

FOR WINTER

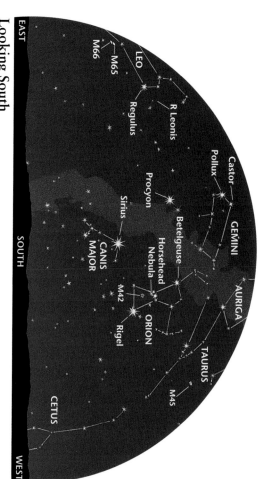

Looking South

The sky is dominated by the bright stars of Orion, the Hunter. Orion is surrounded by Taurus, the Bull; Gemini, the Twins; and Canis Major, the Great Dog. Canis Major contains Sirius—the sky's brightest star.

EAST

SOUTH

WEST

M66

M65

LEO

R Leonis

Regulus

Castor

Pollux

GEMINI

Procyon

Sirius

Betelgeuse

Horsehead
Nebula

CANIS
MAJOR

AURIGA

M42

ORION

Rigel

TAURUS

M45

CETUS

STAR CHARTS

charts for May 15, 9 p.m.

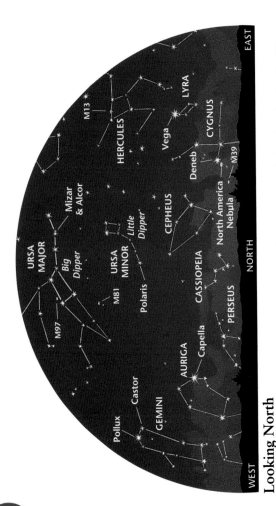

Looking North

The Milky Way forms a band along the horizon. High in the sky is the Big Dipper. Look to the east for the bright, bluish star Vega, in Lyra, the Lyre. To the west are Castor and Pollux, the bright twins of Gemini.

FOR SPRING

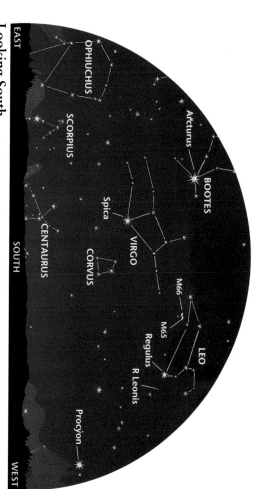

Looking South

High in the sky is Leo, the Lion, with its "backward question mark" shape. Two bright stars stand out in the sky—the white star Spica, in Virgo, the Maiden, and the orange star Arcturus, in Bootes, the Herdsman.

EAST

OPHIUCHUS

SCORPIUS

Arcturus

BOOTES

Spica

VIRGO

CENTAURUS

CORVUS

M66

M65

Regulus

LEO

R Leonis

SOUTH

Procyon

WEST

STAR CHARTS

charts for August 15, 9 p.m.

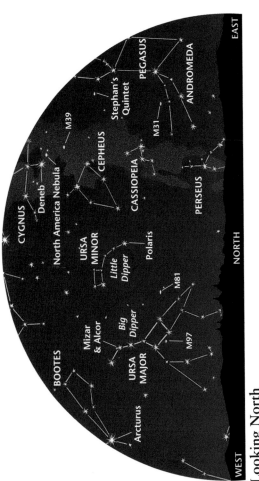

Looking North

The Big Dipper is low in the northwest. Look to the east for the constellation of Pegasus, the Winged Horse, where four bright stars make up the Great Square of Pegasus. Nearby is M31, the Andromeda Galaxy.

FOR SUMMER

Looking South

The Milky Way stretches overhead toward the three stars of the Summer Triangle—Altair and Vega (on this chart) and Deneb (on the Looking North chart). Scorpius, the Scorpion, and Sagittarius, the Archer, are low in the sky.

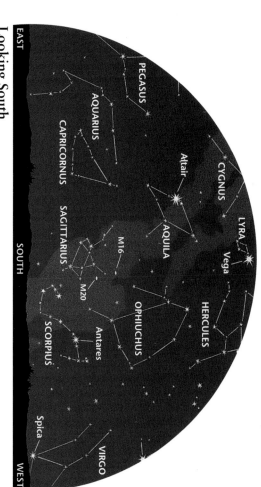

EAST

PEGASUS

AQUARIUS

CAPRICORNUS

CYGNUS

Altair

LYRA

Vega

SAGITTARIUS

AQUILA

M16

M20

HERCULES

OPHIUCHUS

SOUTH

Antares

SCORPIUS

Spica

VIRGO

WEST

STAR CHARTS

charts for November 15, 9 p.m.

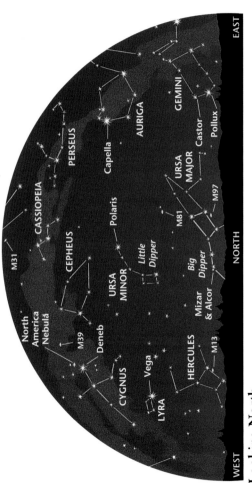

Looking North

The W-shaped constellation of Cassiopeia is high in the sky, while the Big Dipper is low. You can see the cross-shaped constellation of Cygnus, the Swan, in the west, where the Milky Way is crowded with stars.

74

FOR FALL

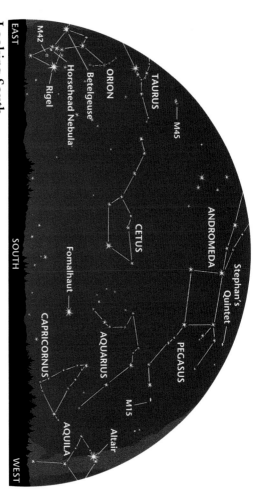

Looking South

The sky has the bright stars of Orion rising in the east. The Great Square of Pegasus is now nearly overhead. Low in the sky is the bright star Fomalhaut—sometimes called the Solitary One because it stands alone.

GLOSSARY

Atmosphere The thin layer of gas surrounding some planets. The air we breathe is part of Earth's atmosphere.

Billion A thousand million. In numerals, it is written as 1,000,000,000.

Constellation One of the 88 official star patterns that make up the entire sky.

Crater A round scar left on a planet or moon where a meteorite has crashed into it.

Crescent A thin curved shape. The Moon is crescent-shaped when less than half of its disk is lit by the Sun.

Disk The flat, round shape you see when looking at a planet or moon.

Eclipse When a moon or planet passes in front of the Sun, blocking its light from another moon or planet, such as Earth.

Galaxy An enormous group of billions of stars and clouds of gas and dust, held together by the force of gravity.

Gas A more thinly packed substance than a liquid or a solid. The air we breathe is a gas.

Gravity The force that holds planets and moons in orbit. Gravity is also the force that holds you on the ground.

Horizon The imaginary line where the ground seems to meet the sky.

Light year The distance that a light beam travels through space in a year—about 6,000 billion miles.

Moon A natural object that orbits a planet.

Orbit The pathway that one object, such as the Moon, follows around another object, such as Earth.

Planet A large object, such as Mars, that orbits a star, such as the Sun. A planet can be seen only because of reflected starlight.

Solar system A group of planets, comets, asteroids, and dust orbiting a central star.

Star A large ball of gas that produces light and heat. The Sun is a star.

Universe All the galaxies, stars, moons, planets, and dust scattered throughout all space. Everything!

INDEX OF
STARS AND
PLANETS

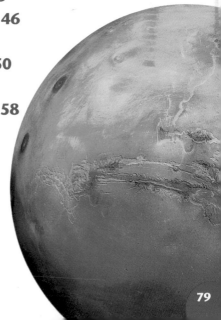

ABOUT THE CONSULTANT

Dr. John O'Byrne has been interested in astronomy all his life and was given his first telescope when he was 12 years old. He turned this into a career by studying physics at the University of Sydney, in Australia. His main expertise is in optical systems used in astronomy, and this has involved him in projects at universities and observatories in Australia and the United States. He is now Senior Lecturer in Physics at the University of Sydney and a secretary of the Astronomical Society of Australia. He is particularly interested in astronomy education. He teaches courses for adults and conducts telescope viewing nights for schools and clubs.

PHOTOGRAPHIC CREDITS

(Key: t = top; b = bottom) **front cover** Austral International/Pictor Uniphoto **back cover** The Photo Library Sydney/NASA/SPL **4** Stock Photos Pty. Ltd./TSM-Mug Shots **5** Weldon Owen **6** National Radio Astronomy/AUI **7** The Photo Library Sydney/NASA/SPL **8** The Photo Library Sydney/David A. Hardy/SPL **9** Stock Photos Pty. Ltd./Mark M. Lawrence **11** National Optical Astronomy Observatories **12** Photo Researchers, Inc./NASA Science Source **15** Comstock **16** Stock Photos Pty. Ltd./Frank Rossotto **18** Stock Photos Pty. Ltd./Stocktrek Photo Agency **20** UCO/Lick Observatory **21** UCO/Lick Observatory **22** The Photo Library Sydney/USGS/SPL **25** Tom Stack & Assoc./NASA **27** Austral International/Pictor Uniphoto **29** The Photo Library Sydney/SPL/NASA **30** Planet Earth Pictures **32** Foto International **33** The Photo Library Sydney/David Hardy/SPL **34** The Photo Library Sydney/Pekka Parviainen/SPL **37** NASA **39** The Photo Library Sydney/Rev. Ronald Royer/SPL **40** Bruce Coleman Limited/Mr. Johnny Johnson **42** The Photo Library Sydney/NASA/SPL **43** REX Features **45** The Photo Library Sydney/John Sanford/SPL **47** Stock Photos Pty. Ltd./Bavaria Bildagentur GMbH **49** Anglo-Australian Telescope Board **51** Visuals Unlimited **53** The Photo Library Sydney/Ronald Royer/SPL **55** Tom Stack & Assoc./Bill & Sally Fletcher **56** Royal Astronomical Society **57** Anglo-Australian Telescope Board **59** The Photo Library Sydney/John Sanford/SPL **61** The Photo Library Sydney/John Sanford/SPL **63** The Photo Library Sydney/John Sanford/SPL **65** The Photo Library Sydney/John Sanford/SPL **67** The Photo Library Sydney/John Sanford/SPL **76t** Stock Photos Pty. Ltd./Frank Rossotto **76b** Pictor Uniphoto/Austral **79** Photo Library Sydney/USGS/SPL.